## DATE DUE

| | |
|---|---|
| JAN 3 0 2003 | OCT 2 4 2011 |
| FEB 1 5 2003 | |
| APR 2 1 2003 | OCT 2 4 2011 |
| SEP 1 1 2003 | JUL 2 2015 |
| MAR 1 8 2004 | AUG 0 9 2013 |
| AUG 2 3 2004 | OCT 0 6 2014 |
| FEB 1 9 2005 | |
| MAY 2 5 2005 | |
| JUL 1 5 2015 | |
| OCT 2 9 2005 | NOV 3 2015 |
| FEB 2 1 2006 | NOV 2 8 2015 |
| NOV 0 6 2007 | DEC 2 2 2015 |
| APR 1 2 2008 | |
| MAY 2 4 2008 | |

Demco, Inc. 38-293

# The
# Moon

# The
# Moon

## Michael George

THE CHILD'S WORLD, INC.

**Library of Congress Cataloging-in-Publication Data**
George, Michael, 1964–
The Moon/Michael George.
p. cm.
Includes index.
Summary: Text and photographs examine the origins, geology, and
exploration of Earth's nearest neighbor in space.
ISBN 1-56766-386-9 (alk. paper)
1. Moon—Juvenile literature. [1. Moon.] I. Title.
QB582.G46 1997
523.3—dc21 96-46675
CIP
AC

## Photo Credits

COMSTOCK/COMSTOCK, Inc: 9, 30
COMSTOCK: Russ Kinne: 15, 24
NASA: cover, 6, 10, 13, 16, 19, 26, 29
Patrick Cone: 2
Photri, Inc: 20, 23

## On the Cover...

Front Cover: The Moon is a beautiful sight in the night sky.
Page 2: : Sometimes the Moon can be seen during the day.

# Table of Contents

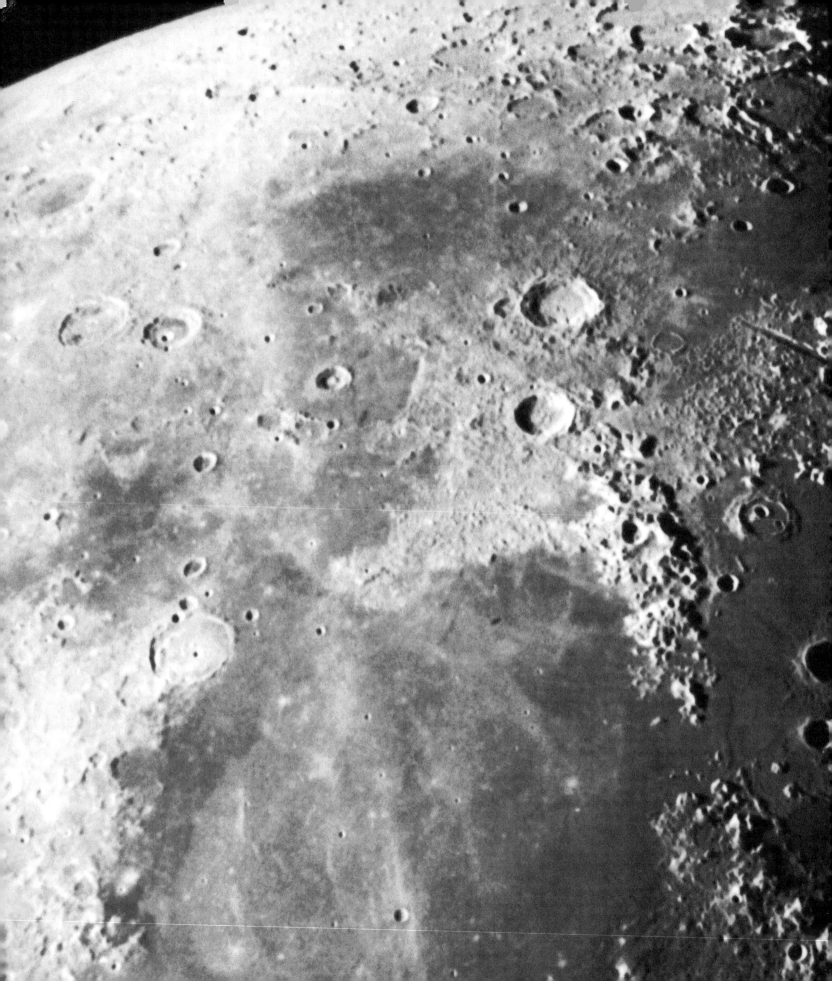

Have you ever dreamed of living on another world? If so, you have probably imagined the strange creatures that would live there. Perhaps bug-eyed monsters live on your imaginary planet. Or maybe the world is covered by meat-eating plants that bloom at night.

Some parts of the Moon look like strange worlds.

Somewhere there might be worlds like this, but scientists have yet to find one. Our closest neighbor in space is the Moon. It is about 240,000 miles from Earth. The Moon is a strange world filled with many unusual sights. However, the Moon is not as inviting a world as you might imagine.

The Moon shines over the desert.

Like Earth, the Moon is a huge ball of rock. The Moon circles around Earth, just as Earth circles around the Sun. When something makes a circle around something else, it makes an **orbit**. The Moon takes about 28 days to orbit once around Earth.

Earth's moon is one of the largest moons in our **solar system**. Our solar system includes the Sun and the nine planets that circle around it. Earth's Moon is about 2,000 miles wide. That is about one-fourth as wide as Earth. If you could ride your bike around the world, it might take you a year. It would take you only a few months to pedal around the Moon.

It is easy to see that the Moon is much smaller than Earth.

Earth is not the only planet that has a moon. Most of the other planets have moons, too. In fact, some planets have more than one. Saturn has the most of all. If you lived on Saturn, you could see 22 different moons rise every day!

Earth's Moon is the only moon that people have visited. In 1969, the United States sent three men to the Moon. They walked on the Moon's surface and took pictures. The men also collected rocks and dust to bring back to Earth. The information they gathered helped us learn more about the Moon.

This astronaut is walking on the surface of the Moon.

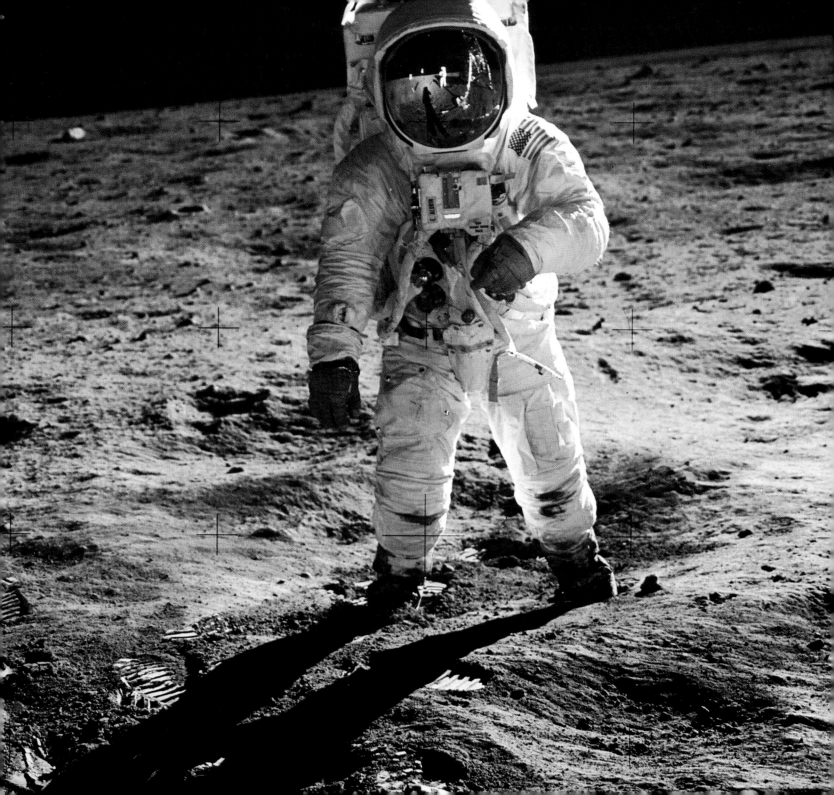

Although the Moon is the brightest object in our night sky, it does not shine on its own. Instead, it is lit by light from the Sun. From Earth, we can see only half of the Moon—the side that faces the Sun. The side that faces away from the Sun is always dark.

The Moon in this picture looks bright, but the other side is completely dark.

If you watch the Moon night after night, you will see it slowly changing shape. One night it will look like a full circle. A few weeks later it will look like a thin sliver. These changes in the Moon's shape are called **phases**.

The Moon doesn't actually change shape each night. Instead, we just see different amounts of its sunlit surface. When Earth blocks the sun's light, the Moon blends in with the blackness of space.

This phase of the Moon is called *crescent*.

## Gravity on the Moon

Life on the Moon would be very different from life on Earth. For one thing, the Moon's **gravity** is much weaker than Earth's. Gravity is the force that pulls things toward any planet or moon. Gravity keeps your feet on the ground and gives you weight. If you weigh 60 pounds on our planet, you would weigh only ten pounds on the Moon. If you can hop over a rock on Earth, you could leap over a car on the Moon!

With the Moon's gravity, it is easy for this astronaut to hop around quickly.

# Daytime on the Moon

If you visited the Moon, you would also have to get used to the length of a day. A day on the Moon is almost 700 hours long! That is because the Moon has 14 Earth-days of sunshine and then 14 Earth-days of darkness. Just think of everything you could do in a day if you lived on the Moon!

Every day on the Moon is exactly like the day before. It is never cloudy and it never rains. The daytime temperature soars to over 200 degrees. When the Sun finally sets, the temperature drops. During the long night, it may drop to 250 degrees below zero!

Every day on the Moon is exactly the same.

# The Moon's Surface

Compared to Earth, the Moon is very bare. Large holes called **craters** take up much of the Moon's surface. Everything is covered with a fine, gray dust. The craters that dot the Moon's surface are very old. Scientists think most of them formed about 4 billion years ago. They were created as large rocks called **meteoroids** hit the Moon. Each crash destroyed the meteoroid but left a pothole on the surface of the Moon.

These craters were formed by meteoroids that crashed into the Moon.

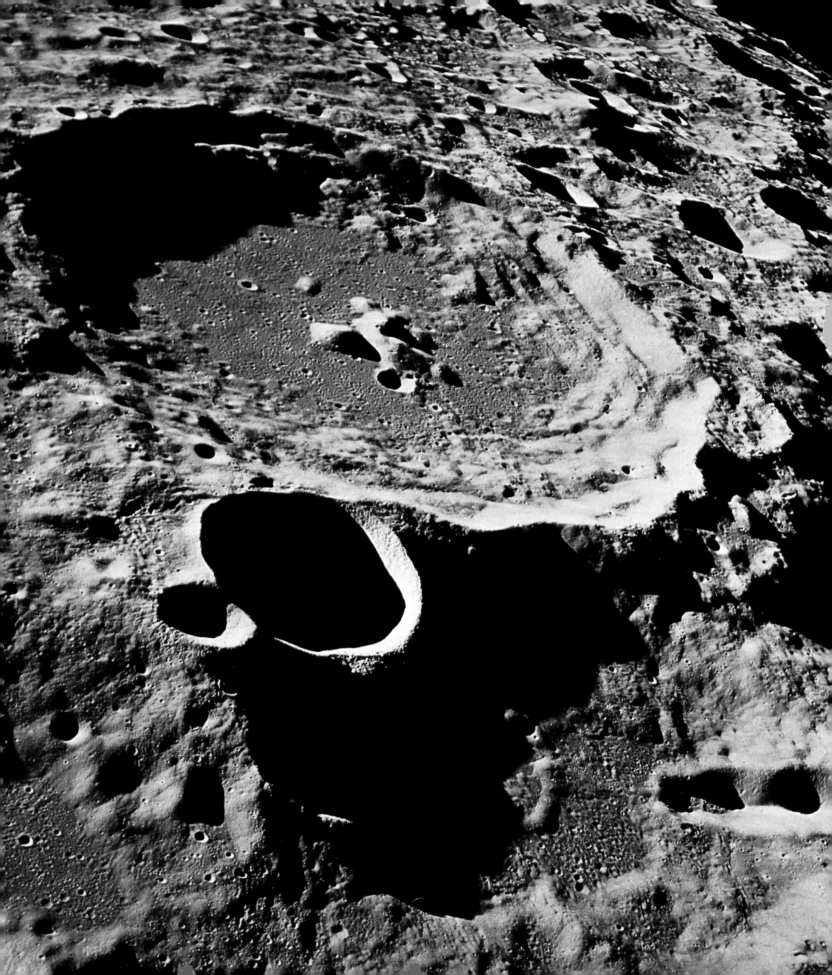

Craters cover most of the Moon's surface, but other areas are smooth and crater-free. From Earth, these sections look like large, dark patches. They are called **maria** (MA–ree–uh).

Like the craters, the maria formed billions of years ago when the Moon had volcanoes. The volcanoes spat ashes and **lava**, or melted rock, into the sky. The lava flowed onto low areas, covering the Moon's cratered surface. When the lava hardened, it left the dark, smooth maria. Since then, few new craters have formed. The maria remain smooth to this day.

The Moon's maria look like dark patches.

Certainly, the Moon is different from Earth. The biggest difference is that there is no life on the Moon. Earth is covered with plants and animals, but the Moon has no life at all. There is no air to breathe. There are no green trees, buzzing insects, or singing birds. There aren't any bug-eyed monsters or meat-eating plants, either. The Moon's surface is lifeless, silent, and still.

Since there isn't any air or water, nothing can live on the Moon.

## The Future

One day we might build cities on the Moon. Then people could live and work on the Moon for long periods of time. They would live in buildings called **space stations**. The space stations would have air so people could breathe. They would also protect people from the Moon's hot days and frozen nights. Maybe one day YOU will live on the Moon!

Maybe you can leave your footprint on the Moon like this astronaut did.

For now, the Moon is a bare, lifeless world. The ground is gray, the sky is black, and the surface is lonely. There are no blue oceans, green fields, or red flowers. Even so, the Moon will always be a beautiful sight in the night sky.

The Moon shines over the ocean.

# Glossary

**craters (KRAY–terz)**
Craters are potholes on the surface of the Moon. They formed long ago when meteoroids crashed into the Moon.

**gravity (GRA–vih–tee)**
Gravity is the force that pulls things toward a planet or moon. The Moon's gravity is much weaker than Earth's.

**lava (LA–vuh)**
Lava is hot, melted rock that comes from inside a planet or moon. Long ago, lava spilled onto the surface of the Moon.

**maria (MA–ree–uh)**
Maria are the smooth, dark areas on the surface of the Moon. They were formed long ago by hot, flowing lava.

**meteoroids (MEE–tee–or–oydz)**
Meteoroids are rocks that float in outer space. When meteoroids crashed into the Moon long ago, they left huge craters.

**orbit (OR–bit)**
When something makes an orbit, it circles around something else. The Moon orbits around Earth.

**phases (FAY–zez)**
The changes in the Moon's shape are called phases. The Moon looks different depending on how much of its surface is in sunlight.

**solar system (SOH–ler SIS–tem)**
A solar system is a star and the planets that circle around it. Earth is a planet, but the Moon is not.

**space stations (SPACE STAY–shunz)**
Space stations are buildings in outer space that people might live in someday. Space stations would provide air and protect people from the temperatures of space.

# Index